Donated to
SAINT PAUL PUBLIC LIBRARY

Too Much Trash!

By Fay Robinson

Consultants
Robert L. Hillerich, Professor Emeritus,
Bowling Green State University, Bowling Green, Ohio;
Consultant, Pinellas County Schools, Florida

Lynne Kepler, Educational Consultant

CHILDRENS PRESS®
CHICAGO

Design by Herman Adler Design Group
Photo Research by Feldman & Associates, Inc.

Library of Congress Cataloging-in-Publication Data

Robinson, Fay.
     Too much trash! / by Fay Robinson.
         p. cm. – (Rookie read-about science)
     ISBN 0-516-06042-2
     1. Refuse and refuse disposal—Juvenile literature. 2. Litter
(Trash)—Juvenile literature. [1. Refuse and refuse disposal.
2. Litter (Trash)] I. Title. II. Series.
TD792.R63   1995
363.72'8–dc20   95-5560
                                                                        CIP
                                                                        AC

Have you ever thought
about how many things
you throw out each day?

4

At lunch alone, you may throw away your milk carton, a plastic sandwich bag, a dessert wrapper, and an apple core.

Imagine that every kid from every school throws away the same amount. That's a lot of trash!

Did you ever wonder where it all goes? First, trash from your school probably gets loaded into large containers called dumpsters.

Workers come by in garbage trucks to take the trash away.

In many areas, they take
it to a landfill — a large
piece of land that has been
set aside just for trash.

At the end of each day,
bulldozers pack down
all the trash.

Then a layer of dirt is spread over it. These steps keep the trash from blowing around and help keep animals away.

Every day the landfill
grows taller and taller
as more layers of trash
and dirt are added.

Eventually, the landfill has all the trash it can hold. When landfills are full, they can be turned into parks.

Where does trash go when a landfill is full? It goes to another landfill. And when that one is full, it goes to another one.

That might sound easy, but some landfills have a lot of problems. Harmful chemicals may leak into the ground and air near a landfill.

And landfills take up a lot of space — we're running out of room!

15

Some areas have open
dumps instead of landfills.

Dumps are ugly and smelly. They attract unwanted animals.

Other areas burn their trash in huge incinerators. One good thing about incinerators is that the heat they create can be used to heat nearby homes.

The problem with incinerators is that there are poisons in the smoke and ash they leave behind.

Did you ever think that trash caused this much trouble?

21

One of the best ways to help is to recycle. When you recycle something, all of it or part of it can be used again.

In many areas, recycling trucks pick up cans, bottles, paper, and plastics from people's homes.

ONLY
WHITE
OFFICE PAPER
PLEASE!

Or people can bring
things to the recycling
center themselves.

Each material is shipped
to factories where new
bottles, paper, plastics,
or cans are made.

Another way to help is to reuse things. Here are some ideas:

- Use both sides of a piece of paper.
- Use egg cartons, boxes, and empty paper-towel rolls for art projects.
- Reuse plastic and paper bags.
- Use cloth napkins instead of paper ones.

- Give away old toys
  and clothes instead
  of throwing them out.

Can you think of anything else you can do?

Now that you know what a big problem trash is, tell your friends! Everyone can help!

Words You Know

trash   landfill

recycling

dumpster

open dump

bulldozer

incinerator

31

Index

About the Author

Fay Robinson is an early childhood specialist who lives and works in the Chicago area. She received a bachelor's degree in Child Study from Tufts University and a master's degree in Education from Northwestern University. She has taught preschool and elementary children and is the author of several picture books.

Photo Credits

H. Armstrong Roberts – 21; ©P. Degginger, 15; ©Geisser, 16, 31 (top right)

©Norma Morrison – 3

PhotoEdit – ©LA Aboretum, 12; ©Myrleen Cate, 27

Photri – ©Bachmann, 24, 30 (bottom)

Tom Stack & Associates – ©Thomas Kitchin, 8, 10, 30 (top), 31 (bottom left)

Tony Stone Images – ©Arthur Tilley, Cover; ©Mark Segal, 4; ©David Woodfall, 9; ©Peter Cade, 11; ©Marc PoKempner, 29

Valan – ©François Morneau, 17; ©Kennon Cooke, 18, 31 (bottom right); ©V. Wilkinson, 23

Visuals Unlimited – ©Arthur R. Hill, 7; ©John D. Cunningham, 31 (top left)

COVER: Bulldozer distributing trash at a landfill